OUT ONE
EAR AND
IN THE
OTHER

BY JOHNNY HART

FAWCETT GOLD MEDAL • NEW YORK

A Fawcett Gold Medal Book
Published by Ballantine Books
Copyright © 1976, 1977 Field Newspaper Syndicate, Inc.

Library of Congress Catalog Card Number: 83-90035

ISBN 0-449-12457-6

Manufactured in the United States of America

First Ballantine Books Edition: October 1983

10 9 8 7 6 5 4 3 2 1

12·3

WHAT DE NATIONS DAT HAVE DE "H" BOMB
WILL BE LIVING IN.

12·6

12-16

A SECRET ORGANIZATION THAT
WORSHIPS THE DEITY "OC".

12·21

12-25

SOMETHING YOU PUT ON A RUSTY MUSK.

12-8

SOMETHING YOU NEVER DO TO A
230-POUND FRAS.

12·9

12-31

1·5

1-7

THIS YEAR I PROMISE
NOT TO INSULT,...

1-11

PIGS AND FUZZBALLS

CON·VERSION

THE FLIM-FLAM SIDE OF THE STORY.

12·10

1-21

1-27

OK, GROG, I'M GOING TO TEACH YOU TO TALK BY THE REWARD SYSTEM.

EVERY TIME YOU GET A WORD RIGHT, I GIVE YOU A KISS. SAVVY?

1.28

SAVVY!

I SEE YOU'RE ANXIOUS TO GET STARTED.

Kurt

12·11

1·31

2.1

2.2

sling'shot *n.*

the last belt you take before you fall off
the barstool and break your arm.

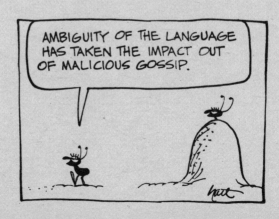

2.8

2·10

2·14

2·16

2·17

2·18

SORRY ABOUT THAT, ACE, ...
JUST HAD THE OL' TOOTSIES
VULCANIZED.

2-22

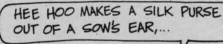

3.1

3.16

3-19

3-21

3·22

3.23

3·29

hart

3·30

42

4.5

4.11

4·12

GRAB LOOP LOOP CINCH

4·15

JUST MY LUCK, I MADE IT THROUGH ANOTHER SUNDOWN.

4·16

factory·seconds' *n.*

WILEY'S
DICTIONARY

4.22

that interminable period of
time between 4:59 and 5 P.M.

WILEY'S
DICTIONARY

hart

3-2

5.3

5-7

WELL, MAUDE, HARV AND I ARE OFF FOR A WEEK OF FISHING!

IT'S ALWAYS YOU AND HARV, HOW COME YOU NEVER TAKE ME?

'CAUSE "SHIRLEY'S LODGE" IS A STAG CAMP.

5-11

HOW ABOUT **SHIRLEY**!

FUNNY,...THAT'S WHAT HARV ALWAYS EXCLAIMS.

hart

5·14

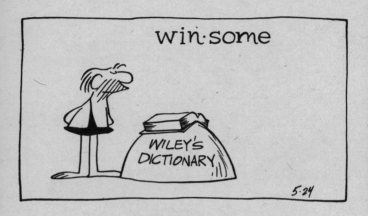

win·some

the first half of a phrase
uttered by a loser.

pol·y·gon

5-26

scratch the crackers.